TOP 10 SECRETS OF SUCCESSFUL G I V I N G

──────── ★ ────────

*How You Can Ensure
Your Gifts Fulfill Your Dreams*

By Ron Robinson & Nicole Hoplin

Published by Young America's Foundation
              F.M. Kirby Freedom Center
              110 Elden Street
              Herndon, Virginia 20170
              800-USA-1776
              www.yaf.org

ISBN: 978-0-615-40886-6

TABLE OF CONTENTS

———————★———————

INTRODUCTION

Where is your money going?

All supporters seek assurance that their gifts are going to legitimate charities. When we give to a charity, we often hope to solve a problem or take advantage of an opportunity on someone else's behalf. Yet we are not present when our gifts are utilized. So, we look for a source of "secondary" approval of our decisions.

Unfortunately, the "drive-by-media" exclusively promote organizations—charity watchdog groups— that evaluate our gifts from a biased worldview. These watchdog groups, with their warped analyses, ultimately discourage conservatives from giving gifts. The watchdogs' bias and government regulations either contribute to gifts being withheld from worthy conservative and like-minded recipients, or, worse from a conservative's perspective, ensure that gifts are sent to institutions that fail to share the donors' beliefs.

Traditional charity ranking organizations are beholden to leftist presuppositions. They reward charities with the highest ratings when those charities:

1.) Use coerced taxpayer dollars (and thus purport to have the smallest fundraising costs).
2.) Rely on "diversity" codes that give preference to racial "bean counting" and quotas in their leadership and among their recipients.
3.) Enforce "equitable" pay scales that most conservatives would never use in their own businesses.

The inference is that only charities that take government funds, support affirmative action, and keep salaries artificially low are worthy of your gifts.

These rating organizations measure "inputs" important to

> ★
>
> "Historically, some of *the* most successful conservative groups refused government funds, hired based on individual merit not on racial quotas, and attracted successful leadership by providing pay comparable to the for-profit sector."

leftist theorists over substantive accomplishments (or outputs). In so doing, the watchdog groups assure fewer gifts flow to free enterprise-oriented, mission-centered, conservative organizations. Yet, historically, some of *the* most successful conservative groups refused government funds, hired based on individual merit not on racial quotas, and attracted successful leadership by providing pay comparable to the for-profit sector.

Nevertheless, gift givers seek objective evidence or a secondary opinion that their generosity is well-placed. Yet conservative and free enterprise-oriented donors do not have access to a charitable rating system that judges an organization's success by how effective it is at advancing freedom.

In our book, *Funding Fathers: The Unsung Heroes of the Conservative Movement,* we document breakthrough gifts that spread free enterprise principles; initiated or sustained successful educational institutions including Hillsdale College, the Heritage Foundation, the Mont Pelerin Society, and Young America's Foundation; formed influential publications and publishing houses including *National Review* and Regnery Publishing; and launched successful careers including those of

Barry Goldwater and Ronald Reagan. These gifts vastly increased freedom at home and abroad.

We note that few of the donors who made these transformational gifts relied upon information from established charitable rating organizations before making their gifts. In fact, it is likely that few, *if any*, of the recipients of these gifts would meet today's standards established by the Better Business Bureau, *Charity Navigator*, *Charity Guide*, or the American Institute of Philanthropy. Regardless, the "unapproved" recipients have become the institutions and leaders who propelled the modern day Conservative Movement to the national forefront.

Short of establishing a new charitable rating organization, *how can you find assurance that your gift is doing as much good as you intended?* We offer a ten-step guide that will assist you in finding worthy recipients of your gifts.

> ★
>
> "Look for charities that
> are already leaders in
> promoting your ideas."

1 GIVE TO CHARITIES THAT ALREADY ADVANCE YOUR IDEAS.

This may seem elementary, but *you are wise to invest in organizations that care enough about your goals to be working towards them already.* In a case we encountered, a supporter wanted to give a property to Young America's Foundation to teach free enterprise ideas. The property had considerable environmental encumbrances and was not suitable for a charity to accept.

When asked if the sponsor might have other property that could be donated to achieve the same educational purpose, the donor indicated he had one worth thirty times the value, but he had already given it to a university to promote free enterprise. When probed about the progress of that free enterprise program and why he had not added funds to it, it became clear the university's use of the supporter's gift had disappointed him. He gave the property because the college was <u>not</u> teaching free enterprise, and he intended for it to establish such a program. Unfortunately, the university never fulfilled the donor's wishes.

The sad truth is that if that university, already well-funded, failed to teach free enterprise to its students to date, then it unlikely is to be a worthy recipient of a major gift to start doing so anew. Evidence that could have warned this supporter included: the university never invited a major free market speaker to deliver its commencement address, it had no free enterprise-oriented economists on its faculty, and there was no hint that the university shared the supporter's values. The school just wanted his money.

Look for charities that are already leaders in promoting *your* ideas. Your gift will add momentum to their tried-and-true teachings. Your gift should <u>not</u> be viewed as leverage to move an institution in a different direction. History has proven it will not work.

EXAMPLE: SPEAKERS SPONSORED BY UNIVERSITIES vs. YOUNG AMERICA'S FOUNDATION

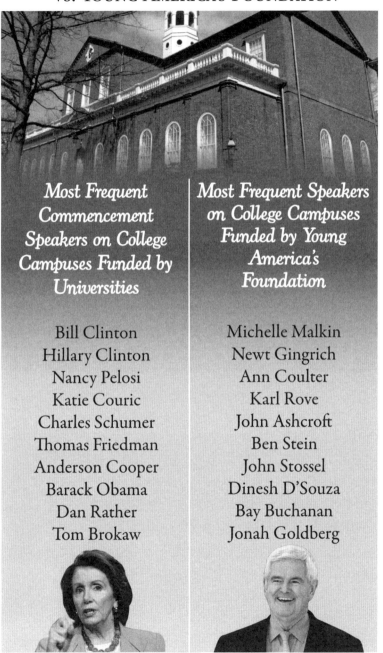

Most Frequent Commencement Speakers on College Campuses Funded by Universities	Most Frequent Speakers on College Campuses Funded by Young America's Foundation
Bill Clinton	Michelle Malkin
Hillary Clinton	Newt Gingrich
Nancy Pelosi	Ann Coulter
Katie Couric	Karl Rove
Charles Schumer	John Ashcroft
Thomas Friedman	Ben Stein
Anderson Cooper	John Stossel
Barack Obama	Dinesh D'Souza
Dan Rather	Bay Buchanan
Tom Brokaw	Jonah Goldberg

2 GET TO KNOW YOUR RECIPIENT ORGANIZATION'S LEADERSHIP.

Visit the organization's headquarters or classrooms to see how it operates. Reputable groups will encourage and desire site visits, and their leaders will welcome a chance to discuss their goals. If a site visit is impractical, call or write the leadership and ask some elementary questions:

1.) How did your leader or CEO become involved in this cause?
2.) What are your great successes?
3.) Who else supports you and why?

Visit the organization's website and see if the issues highlighted are consistent with your goals. Determine whether or not its financial statement or IRS form 990 is easily accessible on its website.

If an institution is too large to be responsive to your desire to get to know its leadership, then it is probably past any "venture capitalism" stage when your gifts might make a decisive difference in the organization's development or programming.

3 Beware of Charitable Rating Groups.

Leftist charities are lavishly funded by coerced taxpayer dollars. You are already supporting them whether you like it or not. Yet, those are the very groups that attack conservative fundraising and suggest fundraising costs are illicit or a waste of support. They already have the federal or state government covering their "fundraising costs," so you do not see their true costs when you evaluate their financial documents. Most conservative and libertarian groups accept no government funds. As a result, at first glance, they might seem to have a higher fundraising percentage than a liberal group.

Again, look for groups that share your values. If a charity is coveting coerced tax dollars—many of those that charity rating groups highly recommend accept government funds—rather than working to earn your voluntary support, then it may be a bad investment, even if it appears to have a more modest fundraising percentage.

The amount an organization spends on fundraising will vary based on its *age* (established groups

★

"Look for groups that share your values."

should have lower fundraising expenses because they often incurred higher percentages in earlier years), whether it receives any *favorable publicity from the mainline media* (most conservative groups have to explain their goals without the media's help), and even whether or not *its fundraisers are active in advancing conservative causes themselves.*

Next, media and "watchdog" groups always overlook investments in conservative organizations made by fundraising firms. Conservative-led fundraising firms, for example those led by Richard Viguerie or Bruce Eberle, have long track records of directing their profits back into Conservative Movement building activities, publications, and conferences. What a state agency or charity rating organization claims is a "fundraising cost" may actually be a vital Movement-building activity, but you would never learn that from the "drive-by" media.

Leftist regulators and "watchdog" groups also rate charities based on racial, gender, and sexual preferences that conservatives find demeaning and irrelevant. Unless you look closely and critically at the "standards" set forth by these watchdog groups, you may miss how biased they are in favor of leftist causes.

4 GIVE INCREMENTALLY.

Do not make a major gift without some experience with the particular charity. Proceed one step at a time. Discover if you are properly thanked with a written receipt. Did you receive a thank you call? For a larger gift, an effective organization provides an accountability report documenting how your support was spent.

We already mentioned a donor who had given a major gift of property (it was worth three million dollars) to a university to establish a free enterprise program. The supporter could have begun with a more modest gift to fund a one-time free enterprise lecture at the college. He would have been able to gauge if the university was willing and able to invite a free market scholar similar to the type of faculty member he hoped to endow. The donor would see how the institution handled his support before he made such a large commitment of his resources.

When you support an organization, you will be more aware of when and how it is mentioned in the conservative media. Is its work reported on in *National Review, Human Events, Washington Times,* or *NewsMax?* Do you notice its spokesmen on talk radio, C-SPAN, or cable news? Do you receive an invitation to its activities? Have you met graduates of its programs? If you only hear of a group from fundraising letters, you may have reason to be skeptical.

5

RELY ON AN ORGANIZATION'S NEWSLETTERS AND WEBSITE IN ADDITION TO ITS FUNDRAISING APPEALS.

Fundraising appeals will tell you what problem or issue a group thinks will garner support. Its newsletter and website will reveal its targeted issues and projects. They may not be identical, but they should be related.

Ask a group for its newsletters, annual report, and its greatest success stories, and you will gain more insight than by relying only on its fundraising appeals for substantive information.

6 ASK OTHERS WHO SHARE YOUR VIEWS WHAT THEY KNOW OF AN ORGANIZATION YOU PLAN TO SUPPORT.

Most credible organizational representatives will not attack or openly criticize a colleague organization, so a direct question to an organization's development officer or leadership usually does not elicit the most complete information. Try a question like this: "If you could not give to your own organization, to which group would you give? Why?" Or, "Share with me your opinion on which groups do the most effective work—give your area of interest (e.g. on Capitol Hill, with young people, on national defense, or to support our troops)?" Or, "Other than your own organization…which groups do you think are most effective in advancing our ideas and why?"

The professional staffs of most conservative organizations know the strengths and weaknesses in the Conservative Movement. Ask for their advice. Often you will receive very insightful answers when you talk to organizational representatives. In addition, fellow conservative donors and conference attendees, especially those who may have been active longer than you, may have useful observations on various organizations.

> "If you are investing
> in a group over time,
> consider joining the
> group at one or more of
> its events."

7 ATTEND A MEETING OF A GROUP YOU PLAN TO HELP.

Almost all major organizations hold conferences
and seminars. If they do not, then ask yourself:
How do they accomplish their mission? If you are
investing in a group over time, consider joining the
group at one or more of its events. You will probably
enjoy the company of like-minded individuals
and appreciate its speakers. You will leave with a
better understanding of the organization you are
supporting, and you will have a chance to meet their
staffs and see how they interact with other supporters
and constituents.

8 DISCARD THE LEFTIST ASSUMPTION THAT SOCIALIST PAY SCALES ARE ASSOCIATED WITH BETTER CHARITIES.

Liberals and socialists are obsessed with leveling all salaries to a common amount. They attack wage differentials, corporate salaries, and, by extension, nonprofits' salaries. In fact, much of the Left's ideology is driven by envy and coveting their neighbors' goods, so it is almost inevitable that liberals evaluate charities by the salaries they pay.

Reviewing overall salaries *alone* may not be a useful tool in deciding where your charity gifts should go. Does the charity rely on a professional staff to coordinate a large group of volunteers? Is the charity a legal defense fund where most of its costs would be expected to pay for lawyers? It would be a *good* benchmark to see such charities pay a substantial portion of their income in salaries.

But should you dismiss an organization when one or more key individuals receive a "large" salary? It is premature to jump to a conclusion without knowing the employees' years of experience, professional qualifications, or other factors considered by the organization's compensation committee. Jim Collins, the business analyst who wrote the mega best seller

Good to Great, suggests reaching a negative conclusion based on a high salary structure is "a well-intentioned idea, but reflects profound confusion between inputs and outputs."

Collins cites Stanford University paying its coaching staff high salaries. "Should we therefore rank Stanford 'less great?'" Collins calls such a conclusion "absurd." Stanford beat all major schools ten consecutive years and had athletes graduating at rates above 80 percent! The key question to ask, according to Collins, is: "How effective do we deliver on our mission and make a distinctive impact, relative to our resources?"

In *Forces for Good: The Six Practices of High-Impact Nonprofits,* authors Leslie Crutchfield and Heather McLeod Grant note, "The Social Sector has inherited an erroneous belief that every penny should go directly to programs rather than overhead, as if programs could deliver themselves."

If salary levels remain important to you, consider two other factors. Inflation makes salaries look deceptively larger over time. To match a $15,000 salary in 1954, it would take a salary of more than $120,000 today. If you recall your salary in years gone by and compare it against a nonprofit's salary scale today, you need to adjust your calculations for inflation.

Finally, nonprofit leaders, by law, have no ownership stake in organizations they help build. They receive no stock options or other incentives. A conservative leader may spend his life helping to build a nonprofit. Yet, the leader will not have an ownership right to pass those assets to his family as he would in a for-profit enterprise.

How much is a 1954 salary worth today, with inflation?

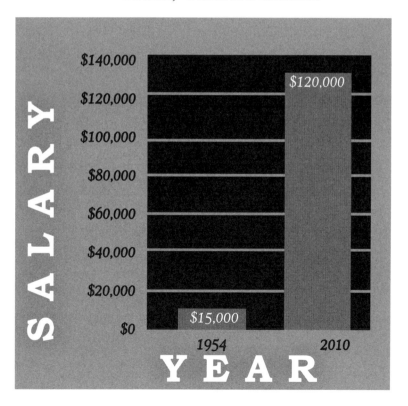

9 RELY ON TRUSTED ENDORSERS OF AN ORGANIZATION.

Can you trust Attorney General Ed Meese, Dr. Walter Williams, Michael Reagan, Michelle Malkin, or a knowledgeable conservative House or Senate Member? Or do you place your trust in anonymous, usually liberal, rating agencies? Many of the great gifts in *Funding Fathers* were made because the donor trusted a Ronald Reagan, a Milton Friedman, or a Bill Buckley.

You should have a higher level of confidence in an organization if a leader "in-the-know" voluntarily endorses the group or gift. Their reputations are on the line, and conservative leaders seldom endorse unknown organizations. This is why the Left seeks to intimidate signers of conservative letters or endorsers of effective conservative organizations. If a conservative leader perseveres through those attacks and tells you that a conservative organization serves a critical purpose, then you have cause to be more confident in your gift to that group.

10 OBSERVE WHICH ORGANIZATIONS THE LEFT ATTACKS.

Leftists are not reliable when they suggest they know best which charities or institutions you should support. However, they are quite reliable in their attacks on the Conservative Movement's most effective organizations. The great recipients studied in *Funding Fathers*—the *Manion Forum*, Barry Goldwater and his *The Conscience of a Conservative,* Ronald Reagan, the Heritage Foundation, Leadership Institute, *National Review,* Hillsdale College, and Young America's Foundation—were frequently under attack.

More recently, George Soros and radical groups such as the Center for American Progress funded attacks on the most effective conservative organizations.

When Bill Clinton, George Soros, and David Halperin organized a major conference to reorganize future leftist youth programs, they cited the success of "groups such as Young

★

"Pay attention to those groups or leaders the Left attacks; they are great clues as to which organizations and individuals are effectively advancing free enterprise, individual liberty, and America's sovereignty."

America's Foundation, the Intercollegiate Studies Institute and the Leadership [Institute]" as their models. That tells you more about which groups are effective than a watchdog organization's ratings. Pay attention to those groups or leaders whom the Left attacks; they are great clues as to which organizations and individuals are effectively advancing free enterprise, individual liberty, and America's sovereignty.

★

"You have a chance to make great gifts that will pass on America's heritage of freedom."

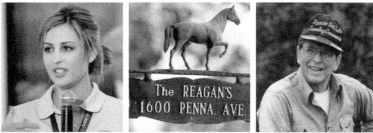

A good example of a transformational gift is the saving of a Presidential property, such as the Reagan Ranch.

CONCLUSION

You have a chance to make great gifts that will pass on America's heritage of freedom. In fact, your involvement is desperately needed if freedom is to be nurtured, protected, and expanded. *Funding Fathers* is about the unsung heroes of the Conservative Movement—individuals who made gifts that transformed America and the world. Those gifts supported Hillsdale College, established free enterprise publications and think-tanks, began the most effective conservative conferences, and launched the public policy career of Ronald Reagan. They helped defeat Communism and kept America safe in perilous times. You enjoy greater freedom today because your predecessors made great gifts. You can do the same.

There is a safe and reliable path to continue that tradition. It is to give gifts to causes that share your values. There are some absolutely time-tested lessons of effective giving, and we are honored to share them with you. We pray you employ them.

If we can provide any additional information or answer your questions, please contact Ron Robinson or Nicole Hoplin of Young America's Foundation at 1-800-USA-1776.